SPORTS FOR SPROUTS

GYMNASTICS

Holly Karapetkova

ROURKE PUBLISHING

Vero Beach, Florida 32964

www.rourkepublishing.com

Photo credits: All photography by Renee Brady for Blue Door Publishing, except Cover © Wendy Nero; Title Page © Wendy Nero, Crystal Kirk, Leah-Anne Thompson, vnosokin, Gerville Hall, Rob Marmion; Page 8 © © Vyacheslav Osokin; Page 12 © Robert J. Daveant; Page 14 © Tony Wear; Sidebar Silhouettes © Sarah Nicholl

Editor: Meg Greve

Cover and page design by Nicola Stratford, Blue Door Publishing

Acknowledgements: Thank you to *Tumbleweeds* (www.tumbleweedsgym.net), Melbourne, Florida, for their assistance on this project

Library of Congress Cataloging-in-Publication Data

Karapetkova, Holly.
  Gymnastics / Holly Karapetkova.
     p. cm. -- (Sports for sprouts)
  ISBN 978-1-60694-325-0 (hard cover)
  ISBN 978-1-60694-825-5 (soft cover)
  ISBN 978-1-60694-566-7 (bilingual)
  1. Gymnastics--Juvenile literature. I. Title.
  GV461.3.K37 2010
  796.44--dc22
                                        2009002258

Printed in the USA

CG/CG

www.rourkepublishing.com - rourke@rourkepublishing.com
Post Office Box 643328 Vero Beach, Florida 32964

2

I am a gymnast.

4

At my gymnastics class, I wear a **leotard**.

We stretch our arms and legs.

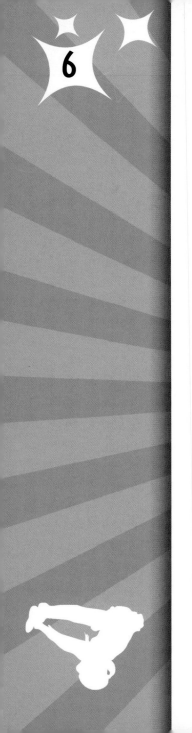

We tumble on
the mats.

We do **somersaults**.

We walk on the balance beam. Don't fall!

15

We flip around
the bars.

We hold our legs in **straddles, tucks, and pikes**.

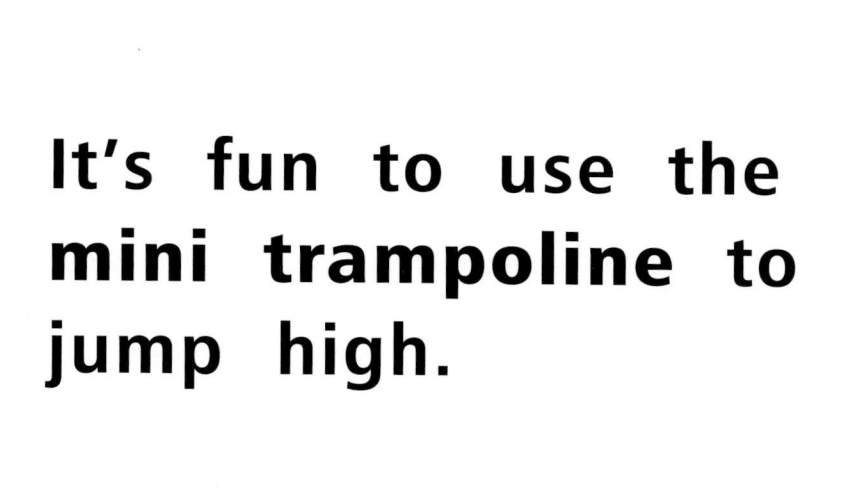

It's fun to use the **mini trampoline** to jump high.

We cheer for each other.
We always try our best!